2 **INTRODUCTION**

4 **THE US PARAS TO PROTECT**
Opening the second front
The paras serve Neptune
German reinforcements in Cotentin _____ 12

15 **'GO, GO, GO... '**
The 101st Airborne in control of the Utah Beach exits... 19
... and the bridges over the Douve _____ 20
The 82nd Division recaptures Sainte-Mère-Église _____ 22
Fierce combat on the Merderet _____ 26
A chaotic German reaction _____ 29

30 **FROM 6TH JUNE TO THE PRESENT DAY**

OREP
EDITIONS

Zone tertiaire de Nonant - 14400 BAYEUX
Ours Tel : 02 31 51 81 31 - Fax: 02 31 51 81 32
info@orepeditions.com - www.orepeditions.com

Editor: Grégory Pique
Graphic design: Éditions OREP
English translation: Heather Inglis

ISBN: 978-2-8151-0399-2 – © Éditions OREP 2018
All rights reserved – Legal deposit: 2nd quarter 2018

Sainte-Mère-É

2

INTRODUCTION

'However, the old question of the wisdom of the airborne operation on the Cherbourg peninsula was not yet fully settled in Air Chief Marshal Leigh-Mallory's mind. Later, on May 30th, he came to me to protest once more against what he termed the 'futile slaughter' of two fine divisions. He believed that the combination of unsuitable landing grounds and anticipated resistance was too great a hazard to overcome. [...] he estimated that among American outfits we would suffer some seventy per cent losses in glider strength and at least fifty per cent in paratrooper strength before the airborne troops could land. Consequently, the divisions would have no remaining tactical power and the attack would not only result in the sacrifice of many thousand men but would be helpless to effect the outcome of the general assault. [...]

It would be difficult to conceive of a more soul-racking problem. If my technical expert was correct, then the planned operation was worse than stubborn folly, because even at the enormous cost predicted we could not gain the principal object of the drop. Moreover, if he was right, it appeared that the attack on Utah Beach was probably hopeless, and this meant that the whole operation suddenly acquired a degree of risk, even foolhardiness, that presaged a gigantic failure, possibly Allied defeat in Europe.'
Dwight Commander-in-Chief of the Allied Forces, Crusade in Europe.

General Eisenhower encouraging the paratroops from the 101st Airborne Division before they boarded for Normandy.

THE US PARAS TO PROTECT UTAH BEACH

OPENING THE SECOND FRONT

On the early hours of the 4th of June 1940, i.e. almost four years to the day before the Normandy Landings, the last ship engaged in Operation Dynamo left Dunkirk with the last remaining Allied escapees on board. The French port was occupied by the German forces the same day.

The British Prime Minister Winston Churchill was to admit, 'Wars are not won by evacuations.' As early as July 1940, in the midst of the Battle of Britain, he ordered for the creation of a Combined Operations department, initially commanded by Admiral Keyes, then by Lord Mountbatten. The initiative was spurred by a realistic aim – not to launch any large-scale operation, but to harass the German troops via surprise attacks along the Atlantic coast.

American propaganda posters to promote troop enlistment, the purchase of war bonds or the construction of landing barges. 'We can! We will! We must!' Roosevelt emphasised. (above, opposite)

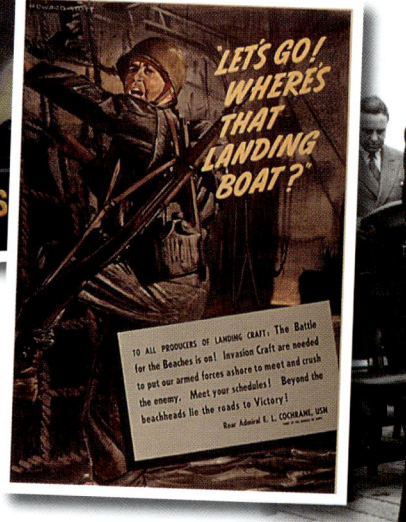

The US President Roosevelt and the British Prime Minister Churchill elaborating the Atlantic Charter aboard the Prince of Wales in August 1941.

The battleships *Tennessee* and *West Virginia* in flames after the surprise attack on Pearl Harbor by the Japanese naval aviation forces.

These raids were to enable the British to gather information on the enemy forces and to destroy strategic structures such as the heavy water plant in Norway or the dry dock in Saint-Nazaire. In August 1942, they even organised a large-scale raid on Dieppe. It was a rehearsal for the major landing which, although it unfortunately failed, nevertheless offered a mine of information that contributed towards the success of the Normandy Landings in June 1944.

However, any hopes for the United Kingdom to return to the Continent alone would be vain. The year 1941 marked a turning point for Churchill. Indeed, on the 22nd of June, the German forces entered the Soviet Union, hence bringing an end to the German-Soviet pact concluded in 1939. Then, on the 7th of December, the surprise Japanese attack on Pearl Harbor brought the United States into the conflict. Yet the British Prime Minister feared that American efforts would be essentially concentrated in the Pacific, to the detriment of the European front.

Churchill very quickly decided to meet with the American President Franklin Roosevelt to put together a joint strategy. The very first conference between the two Allied nations was held late December 1941 – early January 1942, resulting in the 'Germany first' principle. Roosevelt agreed with Churchill's conclusions:

Germany was the most dangerous enemy and was therefore the first to defeat.

War Bonds were to help fund the greatest amphibious operation of all time.

In contrast, the two leaders were quick to diverge on the strategy required to attain their objective. The American military chiefs wanted to attack the German forces on the Continent as quickly as possible, whereas the more experienced British commanders considered a large-scale European operation in 1942 as yet premature. They believed important to use and abuse the enemy; to force it to disperse its troops via 'peripheral' attacks. It was Churchill who initially convinced. Hence, the first extensive amphibious operations were launched in North Africa in 1942, then in Sicily and Italy in 1943.

Despite the Italian surrender in September, the Allied progression in the peninsula was brought to a rapid halt by staunch German resistance relying on a highly favourable defensive terrain.

An operation in Northern Europe became an increasing priority, even if it had never really left the shelf, an interallied staff referred to as the COSSAC (Chief of Staff to the Supreme Allied Commander) commanded by General Morgan having already worked on the plan since 1943. In May, during the Trident Conference held in Washington, the date of 1st May 1944 was set. Then, two months later, during the Quebec Conference, the Allies agreed on the site: the landings would take place in Normandy – sufficiently close to England to be covered by Allied aviation forces, whilst benefiting from lesser protection behind the Atlantic Wall which the Germans had concentrated essentially further north.

Airborne weapons were of recent invention and magnetised many an intrepid man.

General Eisenhower on the front page of *Life* magazine a few days after the landings.

In December 1943, General Eisenhower was appointed Commander of the SHAEF (Supreme Headquarters Allied Expeditionary Force), which integrated the COSSAC. Eisenhower and General Montgomery, who was in charge of land forces, then reviewed the plan elaborated by Morgan's staff. Indeed, they considered that the planned assault, led by three divisions with support from two thirds of an airborne division, would lack in power. Furthermore, Allied logistics comprised a huge enterprise that could never be sufficiently supplied through one single port. Cherbourg was the only easily accessible port in the region chosen for the landings. To capture the town, the Allies decided to extend the zone, adding a beach to the south of Cotentin, which they codenamed Utah Beach. Similarly, for the initial assault, they decided to engage not three but five divisions with support from three airborne divisions entrusted with covering the flanks of the landing zone.

SHAEF's principal commanders (from left to right): General Bradley, in command of the US land forces, General Montgomery, commander of all land forces, Admiral Ramsay, commander of naval units, General Eisenhower, Air Chief Marshal Leigh-Mallory, in charge of airborne forces, hidden by Air Chief Marshal Tedder, Eisenhower's second-in-command and Chief of Staff, General Bedell Smith.

THE PARAS SERVE NEPTUNE

The initial assault, codenamed Neptune, was therefore to be launched in the south of the Cotentin area at the mouth of the River Orne. Utah, the most westerly beach, was particularly suitable for a landing operation. Flat and wide-stretching, it was relatively poorly defended. However, it had the potential to rapidly be transformed into a mouse trap for, immediately behind the shoreline, a vast marshy zone had been maintained by the Germans by blocking waterways with locks and barrages. Only four easy to defend pathways offered exit points from the beach.

It was therefore decided that the 101st Airborne Division would be parachuted in the region of Sainte-Mère-Église, behind this wet zone, with the mission to capture these four exit routes. The division was also to secure the Douve, in order to challenge any counter-attacks from the south.

To reinforce the plan of attack, a second division, the 82nd Airborne, was to be dropped further to the west, in the region of Saint-Sauveur-le-Vicomte, to enable the US troops landed on Utah to quickly isolate the Cotentin peninsula, before taking control of Cherbourg.

The landing was approaching: as the paras left the safety of their camps, black and white stripes were painted on the wings of the planes to distinguish them from enemy craft.

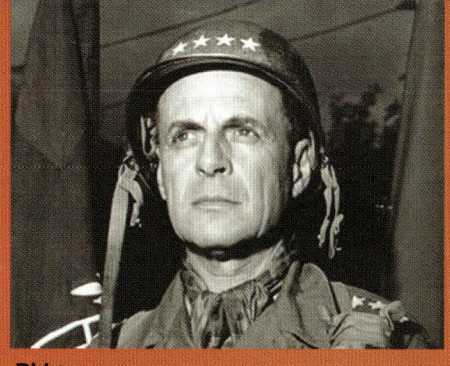

Ridgway
(Major General, Matthew Bunker)

Born in Virginia in 1895, Matthew Ridgway graduated from West Point in 1917, too late to take part in World War I. During the interwar period, he was posted in China, the Philippines, Nicaragua and the United States. In June 1942, he was second-in-command of the 82nd Infantry Division, later to become the first American airborne unit and with which he fought in North Africa, Sicily and Italy. After the Battle of Normandy, he commanded the 18th Airborne Corps. After the war, he was entrusted with several positions of high command, in particular as Supreme Allied Commander in Korea then in Europe in 1952. He was appointed US Army Chief of Staff in 1953, then retired in 1955. He passed away in 1993.

82nd US Airborne Division - Major General Ridgway - Second: *Brigadier General* Gavin			
505th Parachute Infantry Regiment (Col. Ekman)	507th Parachute Infantry Regiment (Col. Millet)	508th Parachute Infantry Regiment (Col. Lindquist)	325th Glider Infantry Regiment (Col. Lewis)
1st Battalion (Major Kellam) killed on 6th June	1st Battalion (Lt Col. Ostberg)	1st Battalion (Lt Col. Batcheller) tué le 6 juin	1st Battalion (Lt Col. Boyd)
2nd Battalion (Lt Col. Vandervoort)	2nd Battalion (Lt Col. Timmes)	2nd Battalion (Lt Col. Shanley)	2nd Battalion (Lt Col. Swenson)
3rd Battalion (Lt Col. Krause)	3rd Battalion (Lt Col. Maloney)	3rd Battalion (Lt Col. Mendez Jr.)	3rd Battalion (Lt Col. Carrell)

Divisional units

4 artillery groups (Colonel March)
319th Glider Field Artillery Battalion
320th Glider Field Artillery Battalion
376th Parachute Field Artillery Battalion
456th Parachute Field Artillery Battalion

1 engineer group
307th Airborne Engineer Battalion

1 anti-aircraft defence group
80th Airborne Anti-aircraft Artillery Battalion

1 medical unit
307th Airborne Medical Company

◀ Corporal Louis Laird, aboard a C-47 and armed with a bazooka during a training exercise.

Taylor (*Major General*, Maxwell Davenport)

Maxwell Taylor was born in Missouri in 1901. As a West Point graduate with a taste for foreign languages, his military career took him abroad, to France and Japan in particular. At the start of the war, he was appointed as General Ridgway's Chief of Staff, within the 82nd Infantry Division. In 1943, Eisenhower sent him as an emissary to talk with the Italian Prime Minister Badoglio to prepare for the 82nd's parachute drop on Rome. However, the Germans were quick to react to the Italian surrender and the operation was cancelled. In March 1944, he was placed in command of the 101st, a position he was to maintain till the end of the war. After taking part in the Korean War and replacing Ridgway as US Army Chief of Staff, he left the army in 1959. However, President Kennedy recalled him to the same position in 1962, when he supervised operations in Vietnam. He permanently retired in 1969 and passed away in 1987.

The 82nd All American was the US Army's first airborne division. It was a practised army corps with previous experience in two parachute operations in Sicily and Italy. This contrasted with the 101st Screaming Eagles for whom the forthcoming operation was the baptism by fire. Both divisions were comprised of voluntary soldiers, some of whom had been drawn by the monthly bonus of $50.

In the spring of 1944, the two divisions were in England, under intensive training pending the future landings. Indeed, this airborne operation – scheduled to be launched by night – required specific preparation. The choice of a nocturnal drop had been spurred by two major considerations. Firstly, a night-time drop would add an element of surprise. Secondly, in the dark, Allied planes would

101st US Airborne Division - Major General Taylor - Second: Brigadier General Pratt			
501st Parachute Infantry Regiment (Col. Johnson)	502nd Parachute Infantry Regiment (Col. Moseley)	506th Parachute Infantry Regiment (Col. Sink)	327th Glider Infantry Regiment (Col. Wear)
1st Battalion (Lt Col. Caroll) killed on 6th June	1st Battalion (Lt Col. Cassidy)	1st Battalion (Lt Col. Turner)	1st Battalion (Lt Col. Salee)
2nd Battalion (Lt Col. Ballard)	2nd Battalion (Lt Col. Chappuis)	2nd Battalion (Lt Col. Strayer)	2nd Battalion (Lt Col. Rouzie)
3rd Battalion (Lt Col. Ewell)	3rd Battalion (Lt Col. Cole)	3rd Battalion (Lt Col. Wolverton) killed on 6th June	3rd Battalion (Lt Col. Allen)
Divisional units			

3 artillery groups (*Brigadier General* McAuliffe)
321st Glider Field Artillery Battalion
907th Glider Field Artillery Battalion
377th Parachute Field Artillery Battalion

1 engineer group
326th Airborne Engineer Battalion

1 anti-aircraft defence group
81st Airborne Anti-aircraft Artillery Battalion

1 medical unit
326th Airborne Medical Company

Paratroops attentively listening to the last instructions before take-off.

Crickets

This simple brass toy was used as a signalling device by paras from the 101st Airborne Division, following an initiative by General Taylor's aide-de-camp. During the night, one click on the cricket was supposed to receive a two-click response to ensure that anyone hiding at the other side of a hedge or an enclosure was indeed a friend and not a foe. If no such response was received, the best bet was to take to one's heels.

be far less visible to the *Flak*, the German anti-aircraft defences that were highly active across the Continent. Previous operations in Sicily and Italy had proved enlightening experiences. In Sicily, some planes had even been shot down by Allied anti-aircraft defences, hence the ingenious idea to paint their fuselage and wings with wide black and white bands, in order to distinguish them from enemy craft. In contrast, a parachute operation by night would inevitably lead to increased troop dispersal for the pilots would have fewer landmarks for them to accurately drop troops. To alleviate the problem, drops were organised in larger and more concentrated groups than during previous operations. In addition, several Pathfinder groups were to jump prior to the major wave in order to mark out Dropping Zones (DZ). To do so, they used holophane lamps to form a large T and Eureka beacons to send radio waves which were intercepted by Rebecca transceivers placed aboard the leader planes. Full-scale exercises were organised to endorse these new techniques. On the 11th and 12th of May 1944, during an exercise codenamed Eagle, the entire 101st Division was dropped in the region of Newbury. Finally, late May, units were bound to secrecy in secured camps where neither further leave nor outing was permitted.

The Douglas C-47 Skytrain

The C-47 was the military version of the DC-3 civilian plane. It was brought into service in 1941, when the United States entered the war. As its name suggests, the Skytrain was the workhorse of the American and Allied air forces. Baptised Dakota by the British, a total of over 10,000 were built during and in the wake of World War II. Both sturdy and reliable, it was used on all fronts, from the North African desert to the Burmese jungle. The C-47 generally transported a stick of eighteen paras with their gear.

Pathfinders from the 505th (82nd Airborne Division) preparing to board for Normandy.

A German platoon in the square next to the church in Sainte-Mère.

GERMAN REINFORCEMENTS IN COTENTIN

The Germans had not remained calmly, arms at the ready, over the months that preceded the landings. As early as 1942, Adolf Hitler published his directive n°40 ordering the construction of a series of defences along the Atlantic coast in order to counter any amphibious operation launched by the Allies. The Organisation Todt, a paramilitary unit, was entrusted with the construction of these fortifications, which gradually comprised what German propaganda referred to as the Atlantic Wall.
Yet, in no way did this line of defence form a continuous wall. It comprised a series of fortified points referred to by the Germans as *Wiederstandnesten* (WN) - resistance nests, established the entire length of the coast. Each nest was supposed to cover a specific sector of beach using antitank guns, mortars and machine guns. Further inland, heavy artillery batteries, with guns often protected within blockhouses, were in charge of sinking any Allied ships that may come to support a landing operation.

Late 1943, Hitler named *Generalfeldmarschall* Erwin Rommel Inspector of the coastal defences that comprised the Atlantic Wall. Rommel was quick to grasp that works in the north of France had made good progress, the German command being convinced that any landing would most likely take place in this sector which was closest to the English shores. Elsewhere, the situation was far from encouraging. Rommel concentrated his efforts on galvanising his troops and reinforcing the defences along the coastline. In particular, he had a series of elements aimed at preventing landing

French labourers working on the construction of the Atlantic Wall.

Vestiges of a Wiederstandnest on Utah Beach.

barges from approaching at high tide set up directly on the beaches: mines, mined stakes, tetrahedrons, etc. This would force the Allies to land at low tide, which would considerably increase the distance the infantrymen would need to cover to reach the shoreline, hence rendering them far more vulnerable to enemy gunfire.

Further inland, beyond the coastal defences, Rommel had units aimed at repelling any successful landing reinforced. Up to 1944, only one division, the *709.Infanterie-Division*, was posted in Cotentin to defend the peninsula. However, in May, the *243. Infanterie-Division*, at the time stationed in south Manche, received orders to take up positions to the west of the peninsula, hence dividing the sector hitherto defended by the *709.Infanterie-Division* in two.

In addition, the *91.Luftlande-Division* was sent to the centre of Cotentin to fend off any parachute drops in the sector. Initially destined to become an airborne unit, it remained an infantry division. Created in January 1944 to take part in operation Tanne in Scandinavia, the division was finally moved to Normandy.

Upon its arrival in the region, its numbers were weak, with around 10,000 men divided into two regiments, rather than the regulatory contingent of 12,000 men. The same applied to its artillery, which was limited

Field Marshal Rommel inspecting the obstacles set on the beaches to prevent the landing barges from approaching the shoreline at high tide.

to forty 105mm *Gebirgshaubitze* guns designed for use in mountainous terrain and requiring different ammunition from standard 105mm guns, which was to rapidly render resupplying problematical.

Similarly, the division's antitank unit only comprised thirty spoiled French tanks, which were totally outdated by 1944. It was nevertheless reinforced by the *Fallschirmjäger-Regiment 6* parachute regiment. Informed of the arrival of these reinforcements in Cotentin, the Allies found themselves obliged to change their plans for the parachute drop. Fearing the 82nd Division may find itself isolated in the region of Saint-Sauveur-le-Vicomte, the Dropping Zones were finally established on either bank of the Merderet, to the west of Sainte-Mère-Église. In turn, the 101st was to be sent to a sector further east, towards the pathways leading to Utah Beach.

On the evening of the 5th of June, as the US paras boarded their planes, the German command was far from on the alert. The poor weather that had hit the zone over the previous two days seemed to be there to stay, presaging no imminent operation. All of the high-ranking officers posted in Normandy and Brittany were therefore invited to Rennes on the 6th of June to attend a *Kriegspiel*, a war game using maps and simulating a potential landing. As the American C-47s flew across the English Channel, half of the German division chiefs and a quarter of their regiment commanders were either on their way or had already arrived in Rennes. General Falley, Chief of the *91.Luftlande-Division*, was also en route when he was alerted by the large number of planes flying overhead. He decided to immediately return to his HQ in Picauville. But he never arrived.

> **The *Fallschirmjäger-Regiment 6***
>
> This parachute regiment, commanded by Baron von der Heydte, was part of the German 2nd German parachute division. In May 1944, the regiment's 3,457 men joined the *91.Luftlande-Division* and were scattered between Périers and Carentan to counter any potential attacks by Allied parachute units. The regiment was alerted as early as 11 pm on the 5th of June and counter-attacked the 101st Airborne's south flank all day on the 6th. Von der Heydte's paras then defended Carentan until they finally withdrew on the 11th of June. The regiment then took part in the battle of the hedgerows to the north of Périers to be virtually annihilated during operation Cobra, which enabled the Americans to break through the German front on the 25th of July.

▲ These infamous 'Rommel's Asparagus', stakes set in the sand by the Germans, have achieved their aim. This Waco glider was dislocated upon landing

'GO, GO, GO... '

On the 4th of June, the weather conditions were so appalling that General Eisenhower decided to postpone the launch of the landing operation by 24 hours.
Finally, the chief meteorological officer Group Captain Stagg who, unlike the Germans, benefited from information from Atlantic weather stations, forecast a milder 36-hour spell as from the 6th of June. Hence, D-Day was set for the 6th.

Lieutenant Colonel Wolverton, chief of the 3/506th adjusting his parachute harness. A few hours later, the suspending ropes became tangled in the branches of a tree and Wolverton became the target of German gunmen. Over 150 bullet wounds were found on his body.

Throughout the day of the 5th, the paratroops joined sixteen airfields where their C-47s awaited them. They rigged themselves out with a range of material and equipment including both a back parachute and an emergency chest parachute. Soon laden with their fifty kilos of gear, many even had trouble moving or boarding their planes unless their buddies offered a helping hand.

Lieutenant Colonel Wolverton's stick posing before the photographer on the afternoon of the 5th of June. Among the group's 17 men, 5 perished including Wolverton and the others were taken prisoner. Most of them managed to escape on the 8th of June.

15

McNiece's Filthy Thirteen

Jake McNiece was a tough guy who had enlisted with the paras to escape American justice. But that did not prevent him from continuing his pranks within the 101st, to such an extent that he was regularly demoted and even bordered on permanent dismissal from his unit. Yet despite all, his sabotage and leadership skills were precious and his superior officer decided to keep him. At Camp Toccoa in Georgia, he was entrusted with a group of twelve men, all of them equally undisciplined. They were soon to be nicknamed the Filthy Thirteen.

As it was preparing to board its C-47 on the 5th of June, the group was immortalised by a team of American cameramen. Just like their chief, they had shaved their hair Mohawk style for fear of catching lice and had painted their faces with the same black and white paint that had just been used on the plane's wings. The team's drop was pretty much in keeping with the rest of the 101st, i.e. scattered, McNiece only locating three of his men and gathering together a few other lost troops. However, he accomplished his mission and destroyed the two wooden bridges over the Douve opposite Brévands then, for five days, defended the bridge leading to Carentan before it was mistakenly destroyed by P-51 Mustang fighters.

Clarence Ware and Charles Plaudo, two of the Filthy Thirteen painting their faces before boarding their plane.

On the evening of the 5th of June, General Eisenhower came to speak with the men from the 502nd Regiment. The dismal warnings he had been given by Air Chief Marshal Leigh-Mallory were still fresh in his mind. The aviator had forecast that the losses among American airborne troops would be such that he believed any such operation should be cancelled.

Eisenhower had decided to maintain the operation; however, no-one knew whether the men he was addressing would still be alive the next day.

With their black faces and already heavily laden, these men have still not attached their two parachutes.

Night has fallen and take-off is imminent for these men from the 101st.

Private Joseph Gorenc from the 506th struggling to board his plane. He was also one of Wolverton's stick. This time, he is boarding for real on his way to Normandy. He has placed his Thompson submachine gun in the straps of his parachute.

Finally, it was time to board and, as from 10:30 pm, the first planes took off at a rate of one every ten seconds. The 433 C-47 planes engaged in mission Albany, transporting some 6,928 men from the 101st Airborne Division, soon joined the 368 planes belonging to the 82nd Division (mission Boston: 6,420 paras) above the English Channel. Then they swerved towards the Channel Islands to approach the Cotentin peninsula from the west. The layers of cloud became increasingly thick and the *Flak* entered into action. The Allied pilots – most of whom were novices – lost their leader and, to avoid enemy fire, tried to zigzag or to rise to higher altitude above the clouds. The red light finally lit up in the cabin and the paras hooked their parachute slings onto the static line, a cable fixed to the top of the craft and running along the middle of the row of paras. At the green light, they jumped towards the unknown.

Another picture of Wolverton's group. They have just boarded the cabin of a C-47, most probably upon the photographer's request for their faces have not yet been painted black, a sign of imminent take off.

17

Adjusting a front and chest parachute required help from a fellow soldier. Such is the case for these men from the 82nd Division.

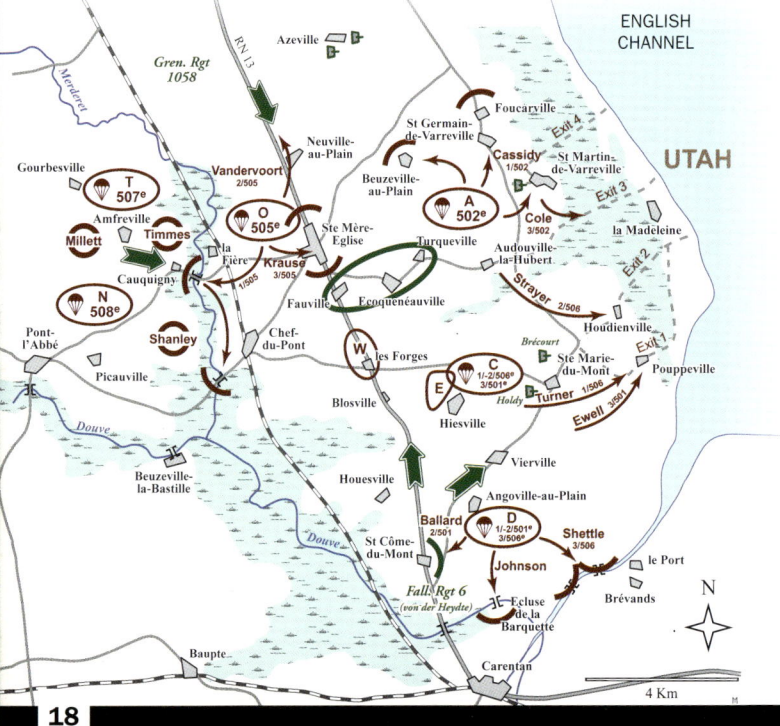

After a twenty to thirty second fall, slowed down by their parachutes, many of those who were lucky enough not to drown in the marshes or to end up hanging from a tree or even a church spire, realised they had not landed on the right spot. The Pathfinders who had been dropped before the vast majority of the paras had also had great trouble finding their Dropping Zones and had, consequently, failed to mark them out as planned, with the exception of DZs C and O. The men were now scattered over a huge zone stretching from north Cotentin to Pointe du Hoc. In such conditions, accomplishing their mission was a seemingly impossible task.

Positions on the evening of 6th of June

Millett Isolated groups

W Glider landing zone

THE 101ST AIRBORNE IN CONTROL OF THE UTAH BEACH EXITS...

Lieutenant Colonel Cassidy successfully reunited two hundred paras from his 1/502nd and took control of the 'XYZ' complex, a group of farms where gunners from the Saint-Martin-de-Varreville battery were stationed. He then established road blocks to the north of the zone in Foucarville and Beuzeville-au-Plain.

In turn, Cole, with his 120 men, most of whom were engaged in the 3/502nd, headed for the Saint-Martin-de-Varreville artillery battery they had received orders to neutralise. However, when he discovered that the guns had been moved after a bombardment, he decided to go straight to Exits 3 and 4, of which he was also to gain control before the 4th US Infantry Division landed on Utah. Exit 3 was neutralised by 7:30 am and Cole informed the 4th Division that Exit 4 was still under German artillery fire and that they best avoid it.

Further south, 220 men commanded by Lieutenant Colonel Strayer (2/506th) set off at 3:30 am towards Exits 1 and 2. However, German machine gunfire slowed down their progress and it was only early in the afternoon that Strayer finally reached Houdienville to join forces with the 4th Infantry.

Further south, with no news from Strayer, Colonel Sink ordered Turner (1/506th) to go to Exit 1 in Pouppeville. After fierce combat and the arrival of reinforcements from Ewell's unit, the exit was finally under control and contact was established at noon with the troops that had landed on Utah.

A famous photograph of men from the 101st on their way to Normandy. Robert Noody, in the centre, jumped with a bazooka. On the 12th of June, he used it to destroy a Panther tank during the Battle of Carentan.

Paratroops from the 101st distributing canned food to the locals in Hiesville.

19

... AND THE BRIDGES OVER THE DOUVE

To the south of the sector covered by the 101st, Johnson's 501st Regiment's mission was to take up position on the River Douve in order to challenge any counter-attack from the south. Initially isolated, Johnson eventually managed to reunite 50 men and captured the Barquette lock, which was devoid of any defences.

The situation was more chaotic for the 3/506th whose battalion chief and second-in-command had both been killed. Captain Shettle had taken over and he marched with 50 men towards the Douve bridges, which they reached at 4:30 am.

James Flanagan and his buddies from the 502nd posing with their trophy after taking control of the XYZ complex, a group of farms under German occupation.

Two hours later, Shettle was to face a violent counter-attack which left him with no choice but to abandon the bridges and to take up position further north, in an attempt to block any further German advance.

Failing the arrival of reinforcements from the 2/501st, Johnson and Shettle were to maintain their uncomfortable position throughout the day of the 6th. Indeed, the battalion had been hindered by an attack by the German 1058th Regiment and Von der Heydte's *Fallschirmjägers* in Les Droueries and Saint Côme-du-Mont.

General Pratt's glider was not the only one to suffer damage when landing. Several airborne troops lie dead before this destroyed Horsa glider.

The Brécourt battery

On the morning of the 6th of June, gunfire struck the beach exits, Exit 2 in particular. The Allies soon located the origin of the attack: a battery equipped with four 105mm guns located in a field on the estate of the Brécourt manor to the north of the village. Colonel Sink, commander of the 506th Parachute Infantry Regiment, then ordered Lieutenant Winters, freshly in command of the Easy Company, to capture the position. With a group of thirteen men, covered by two machine guns, Winters accomplished his task with such tactical genius that his manoeuvre is still taught at West Point. The story of the capture of this battery is told in the second episode of the successful TV series *Band of Brothers*, by Tom Hanks and Steven Spielberg.

Men from the 101st transporting supplies in a hand cart. The one on the right is collecting German grenades.

The same group from the 101st discovering the local beverage: cider.

At 4 am, 52 Waco gliders (mission Chicago) were sent to Landing Zone E to bring heavy equipment to support the 101st Division. However, laden with its cargo, the glider crashed and the division's second-in-command, General Pratt, who was on board, was killed outright. Even if most of the 19 antitank guns, 27 jeeps and 14 tonnes of equipment escaped with little damage, they were not all recovered by the day end, many other gliders remaining under sustained enemy fire. Finally, at 9 pm, 32 Horsa gliders managed perilous landings, bringing with them six guns, 40 vehicles and 19 tonnes of equipment (mission Keokuk).

By the evening of the 6th of June, Taylor was rightfully satisfied. Despite his forces being dispersed - at this point in time only a third of his men were still under his command - all the targets he had been entrusted with were achieved. However, his situation remained precarious and he would need reinforcements to challenge the inevitable counter-attacks.

The Holdy battery

In the hamlet of Holdy, the Germans had established a battery housing four 105mm guns and held by a 50-man garrison. The Allies were unaware of this battery which was a potential threat to the landings on Utah Beach. Discovered by the paras, it was captured by a group commanded by Captains Raudstein and Patch. Convinced that the church in Sainte-Marie-du-Mont was occupied by Germans, the paras used a gun to destroy the spire. However, in truth, men from the 101st had taken refuge inside the church; thankfully, they escaped with more fear than injury. Three of the battery's four guns were eventually destroyed.

THE 82ND DIVISION RECAPTURES SAINTE-MÈRE-ÉGLISE

The 82nd was no better off than the 101st.
The huge troop dispersal during the drop meant that only the men from the 505th Regiment landed more or less within their designated Dropping Zone. However, one stick landed right in the middle of the village of Sainte-Mère-Église, where the village square was illuminated by a burning house. Already on the alert, the German garrison shot at the paras, some of whom ended their fall lifeless amidst the branches of a tree or on top of electricity poles.

These paras have requisitioned a local cart to transport their material through the streets of Sainte-Mère-Église.

Soldiers hunting out hidden snipers inspecting the Lemenicier hardware store.

Elmer Habbs taking a rest at the foot of the signpost marking the entrance to Sainte-Mère-Église on the 7th of June.

Above and below: a team of paratroops trying to dislodge a German sniper entrenched inside the church belfry in Sainte-Mère.

To the west of the village, Lieutenant Colonel Krause (3/505th) managed to rally 150 men and began marching towards Sainte-Mère-Église which they reached at around 4 am. The village was rapidly in Allied hands. Eleven Germans were killed and 30 taken prisoner. Despite a broken ankle, Lieutenant Colonel Vandervoort took command of 400 paras from the 2/505th. They headed northwards and successfully accomplished their mission to establish a road block at Neuville-au-Plain. However, unaware that Sainte-Mère had already been captured, he left Lieutenant

Lieutenant Colonel Vandervoort, chief of the 2/505th suffered a fracture immediately above the ankle when he jumped on the night of the 5th to the 6th of June. He continued to fight over the following days using the crutch that can be seen to his left.

American nurses talking to German prisoners in front of the hospice in Saint-Mère, transformed into a first aid post.

A destroyed German *Sturmgeschütz III* gun at the entrance to Sainte-Mère-Église.

Turnbull's unit in Neuville and headed southwards with the rest of his men. With Krause, he coordinated defences in and around the village.

As from 9 am, Sainte-Mère-Église became the target of German artillery fire and of a series of counter-attacks. Twenty-two civilians lost their lives. To the north, Major Moch, in charge of a battalion from the *91.Luftlande-Division*, failed to regain control of the village, despite support from ten *Panzers*. To the south, the Georgians from the *Ost-batallion 795* were also driven back.

John Steele

When the United States entered the war, John Steele, aged 29, enlisted in the airborne army. He took part in airborne operations in Italy, within the 82nd Division's 505th Regiment. On the night of the 5th to the 6th of June, his stick was accidentally dropped direct in the centre of Sainte-Mère-Église and Steele was wounded in the foot during his descent.

He ended up hanging on the church steeple as the fighting raged throughout the village square. Unable to free himself from his harness, he was taken prisoner two hours later. However, he managed to escape. Steele's misadventure became famous after the publication of the book *The Longest Day* by Cornelius Ryan and, in particular, thanks to its film adaptation. Even if certain details in the film do not retrace the genuine course of events, it contributed towards the event becoming somewhat a legend.

On the 7th of June, paratroops from the 82nd Division recovered horses to patrol through the streets of Sainte-Mère-Église.

Finally, to the east, the men from the *Sturmabteilung AOK 7* were no more successful. At a cost of 44 paras killed and 130 wounded, the road junction established as a priority mission by the 505th was still in American hands, but remained isolated throughout the 6th of June. The Task Force Raff, a special unit comprised of airborne troops aboard 17 Sherman tanks belonging to the 746th Tank Battalion had been entrusted with the mission of landing on Utah Beach and reinforcing Sainte-Mère-Église as quickly as possible.

However, the Germans took full advantage of the natural defences offered by the Normandy bocage and blocked all reinforcements. It was only after a full day of fierce combat that the enemy was finally driven out of the sector.

Infantrymen from the 4th Division, recently landed on Utah Beach, passing near the church in Sainte-Mère.

Two airborne troops from the 325th regiment posing in front of the chapel in Cauquigny, which suffered great damage during the fighting.

FIERCE COMBAT ON THE MERDERET

The first battalion from the 505th was to capture the La Fière bridge over the Merderet, in collaboration with the 507th, dropped to the west of the river. All the night-time attacks on the manor that defended the bridge were in vain. Yet, the survivors among the German garrison finally surrendered at noon and 80 paras, commanded by Captain Schwartzwalder could then cross the bridge and enter Cauquigny, where men from the 2/507th were already in position. They left twenty men in and around the chapel then set off to join forces with Lieutenant Colonel Timmes' troops, entrenched in an orchard to the north of the bridge.

Two Americans inspecting one of the Renault R35 tanks destroyed during the battle for the La Fière bridge. The vehicle had been captured by the Germans after the French defeat in 1940.

Early afternoon, 200 Germans from the 1057th regiment of the *91.Luftlande-Division* attacked the men who had taken refuge in Cauquigny, covered by three tanks, before heading for the bridge. Thanks to antitank gunfire and two bazookas, the three *Panzers* were finally destroyed and the Germans withdrew. The paras had lost twenty of their men and 150 were wounded.

It took a further three days of deadly combat before the La Fière bridge was finally secured. Further south, Lieutenant Colonel Ostberg led his 100 paras to Chef-du-Pont which they reached at 10 am. With his counterpart, Maloney, he secured the eastern bridge entrance, however failed to drive out the Germans who were entrenched on the opposite bank. The situation led to the vast majority of the paras retreating from the bridge, only 34 remaining. They nevertheless succeeded in countering the German attacks and finally taking control of the bridge, thanks to the providential arrival of around a hundred buddies equipped with an antitank gun.

Throughout the 6th of June, the situation to the west of the Merderet remained extremely chaotic. The 507th and 508th regiment drops had been highly inaccurate and many men had no choice but to fend for themselves. Lieutenant Colonel Shanley finally managed to rally some 300 men together; however, they failed to destroy the bridges at Beuzeville-la-Bastille and Étienville, near Pont-l'Abbé. He therefore decided to entrench his troops on Hill 30 overlooking the marshes. Timmes did likewise to the north of Cauquigny with 120 men and Millett with 400 paras to the west of Amfreville. They were subjected to German attacks and artillery fire for two days.

At 1:50 am, 52 gliders loaded with material were sent to support the paras (mission Detroit).

Only 37 landed on Landing Zone Zero at around 4 am. Although the Americans had only lost three men, a vast share of the equipment had been destroyed or dispersed. Between 9 and 11 pm, a further 176 were scheduled to land on Landing Zone W. To avoid

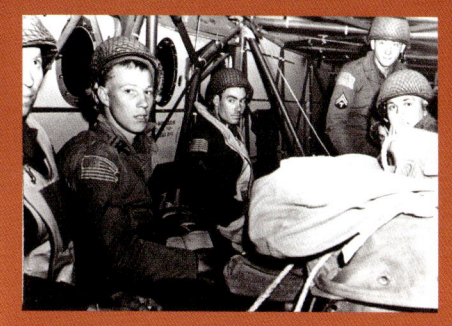

GLIDERS

The main drawback facing parachute troops was the lack of heavy equipment. To compensate, special gliders were designed not only for troop transport but also to bring in material, jeeps and artillery. The Americans used two models: the Waco, built in the United States and the British-made Horsa. Designed around a canvas-covered metal frame for the Waco and a wood frame for the Horsa, they were relatively fragile and many were destroyed or severely damaged during landing. A total of 512 gliders were used in support of the US paras on the 6th and 7th of June.

American paratroops passing by the wreck of a French Hotchkiss tank captured by the Germans in 1940.

27

accidents, they were to land over four successive waves. Once more, many suffered extensive damage. Half of the gliders were destroyed and 48 men were killed. Furthermore, by the evening of the 6th of June, Landing Zone W was under enemy fire and the majority of the airborne troops there preferred to go into hiding for the night rather than try to unload their gliders.

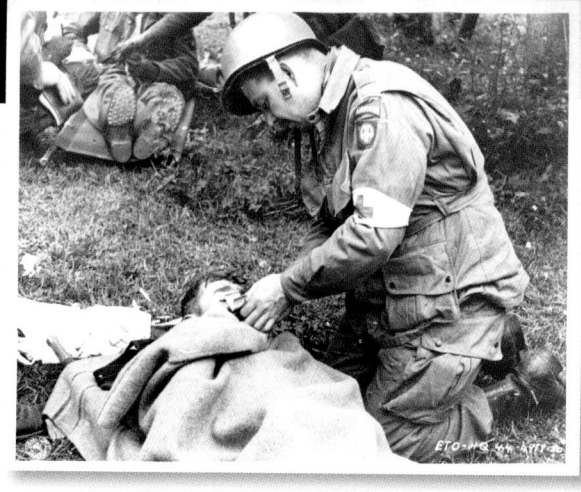

By dusk on D-Day, Ridgway only had 2,000 men under his command. However, despite considerable troop dispersal, the major targets had been met: Sainte-Mère-Église was under control, even if it remained encircled, and the La Fière and Chef-du-Pont bridges were in American hands even if the troops were as yet unable to advance beyond the Merderet. Thus, Ridgway devoted the following days to consolidating his division's positions.

No distinction between friend or foe for this nurse from the 508th offering a wounded German soldier a cigarette.

The counterveneer of this Horsa glider failed to withstand the shock of the landing. The hedgerows of the Normandy bocage became deadly obstacles for the gliders as they landed, sometimes at 100km/h.

This poor parachutist from the 82nd Division was unable to untangle his way out of his parachute ropes and drowned in the marshes around the dropping zones.

A CHAOTIC GERMAN REACTION

The dispersed parachute drops had largely complicated the task facing the US paras and had left certain units in precarious situations, in particular those who were isolated to the west of the Merderet. *In contrast, the landings had disconcerted the German command by preventing it from drawing a clear picture of the Allied objectives.*

In addition, given the poor weather forecast, the operation's mere launch had surprised the Germans. As previously mentioned, several unit chiefs were in or on their way to Rennes to attend a *Kriegspiel*. General Falley, in command of the *91.Luftlande-Division* had finally decided to turn back and return to his HQ in Picauville. A few miles from his destination, he fell under the bullets of an American patrol commanded by Lieutenant Brannen. The principal German unit capable of controlling the American parachute drop was now deprived of its chief.

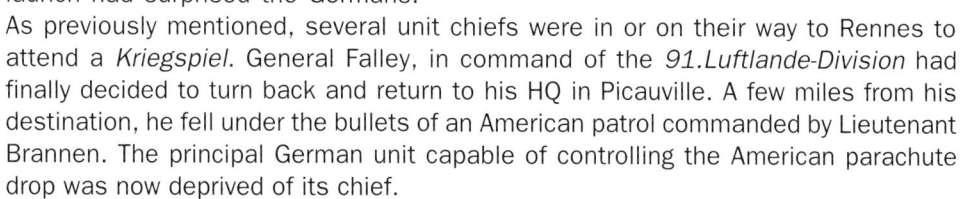

In turn, Von der Heydte's *Fallschirmjäger Regiment 6*, whose men were scattered the breadth of the Cotentin peninsula, was unable to reunite its forces to organise any efficient counter-attack. Over the days to follow, Von der Heydte rallied his regiment around Carentan and steadfastly defended the town.

Finally, at 3 am, General Marcks, in command of the *84.Korps* comprising all forces in charge of countering the landed enemy ranks, ordered for Meyer's *Kamfgruppe* from the *352.Infanterie-Division* to counter-attack the paras. However, after the Americans had landed on Omaha Beach and the British on Gold, Meyer was redirected towards the beaches. Hence, throughout the day of the 6th of June, the American paras were to face no large-scale counter-attack.

General Falley, chief of the 91. Luftlande-Division, was on his way to a kriegspiel in Rennes when he turned back, alerted by the many planes flying overhead. He was killed in an ambush near Picauville.

FROM 6TH JUNE TO THE PRESENT DAY

After the 6th of June, the American airborne units were to suffer a long wait before returning to England. They continued to fight bitterly for over a month. The 101st was to face Von der Heydte's *Fallschirmjäger* for the recapture of Carentan, only in Allied hands on the 12th of June, but henceforth offering a link between Utah and Omaha.

The division was repatriated on the 10th of July 1944 after losing 3,836 men (killed, wounded, unaccounted for or taken prisoner).

This German prisoner has been seated at the front of an 82nd Division jeep as it drives through the streets of liberated Sainte-Mère-Église. Could he be used as a human shield?

▲ A group of nurses posing with a swastika flag taken from the enemy during the liberation of Orglandes on the 17th of June. The two men on the right are Lieutenants Beaudin and Lehman (3/508th). They have just been released after 10 days in captivity. Lehman was killed near La Poterie on the 4th of July.

Paras from the 101st fraternising with the locals in Cotentin.

In turn, the 82nd initially fought to consolidate its positions to the west of Merderet, then contributed towards the operations that led to isolating the Cotentin peninsula.
It then took part in the fierce combat that raged amidst the Normandy bocage, in the La Haye-du-Puits sector. The division was withdrawn from the front from the 10th to the 14th of July, after sustaining 5,060 losses. Today, the area where the US paras were dropped is very much the same as it was in 1944, with its marshes and canals. Several monuments remind visitors of the terrible battles that were waged on these damp landscapes. Several villages are home to steles in memory of the units that contributed towards their liberation.

One of the most famous photographs of an American parachutist, published on the front page *of Life*. Lieutenant Kelso Horne from the 508th, posing for the photographer in the Saint-Sauveur-le-Vicomte sector in June. He was seriously wounded on the 4th of July during the battle to recapture La Haye-du-Puits. He took part in the Ardennes campaign and survived the war.

In 1947, a Norman country woman contemplating the graves in Sainte-Mère-Église's cemetery n°2.

Iron Mike now stands above the La Fière bridge, the theatre of three days of deadly combat.

The most famous among them is most likely Iron Mike, a military statue overlooking the La Fière bridge. In a similar style, visitors can also admire the monument in Sainte-Marie-du-Mont, erected in honour of Lieutenant Richard Winters whose heroism led to the capture of the Brécourt battery. In Hiesville, they can also contemplate the stele that commemorates the loss of General Pratt, killed aboard his glider.

Two museums also welcome visitors to offer them a delve into the atmosphere that reigned on the night the paras landed.

In Sainte-Mère-Église, the Airborne Museum's two buildings house a genuine C-47 and a Waco glider. The 'Operation Neptune' exhibition area offers visitors an immersive view inside the paras' plane or amidst the marshes. A few miles from there, in Carentan, they can also discover what it felt like to fly to Normandy aboard a C-47 thanks to the flight simulator at the D-Day Experience, a museum housed in the very building where the US paras faced the German defenders until the 8th of June 1944. Finally, in Sainte-Mère-Église, three monuments mark the spots of the temporary cemeteries established around the village from June 1944 to 1948: one to the west, one to the east and the third, further south in Blosville-Carquebut.

The Airborne Museum located right next to the church in Sainte-Mère-Église offers an immersive insight into the daily lives of the American parachutists.

A total of around 14,000 American soldiers were buried in these three cemeteries. In 1948, their bodies were finally repatriated to the United States or transferred to the war cemeteries in Colleville-sur-Mer and Saint-James.
Whether they survived or were buried alongside their buddies, the American paras had granted the chief of the 501st Regiment Colonel Johnson his wish. On the evening of the 5th of June, he had harangued them, 'We have worked hard together, sweated together, we have trained together, but what we are going to do tonight will go down in History.' Mission accomplished.

Sainte-Mère-Église

6th June 1944 in the Cotentin peninsula. Thousands of huge white petals opened amidst the dark of night. Thirteen thousand American paratroops were dropped in the sector to the west of the Normandy landing zone. However, many fell far from their targets. It took several hours for some of them to finally connect with a buddy or an army group, that was equally astray. Nevertheless, all the missions entrusted to the parachute units were successfully accomplished. The 101st Airborne Division managed to cover the area inland of Utah Beach, whilst the 82nd Airborne Division controlled Sainte-Mère-Église and the surrounding area. Yet, the American positions remained extremely fragile, in particular at the La Fière bridge. Welcome reinforcements were landed on Utah as from 6:30am. Then the US paras embarked on a month and a half of deadly combat amidst the marshes and the Normandy Bocage.

OREP EDITIONS

ISBN 978-2-8151-0400-5

www.orepeditions.com
Price: €5.70

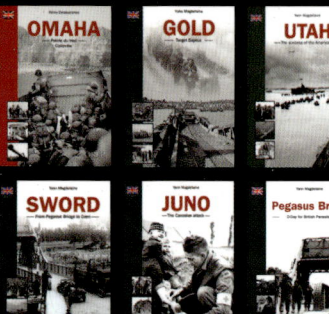

£ 6 60

in the same collection

OMAHA GOLD UTAH
SWORD JUNO Pegasus Bridge